from **TURTLE ISLAND** *to* **GAZA**

MINGLING VOICES
Series editor: Manijeh Mannani

Give us wholeness, for we are broken.
But who are we asking, and why do we ask?
                                        —Phyllis Webb

Mingling Voices invites the work of writers who challenge boundaries, both literary and cultural. The series issues a reminder that literature is not obligated to behave in particular ways; rather, it can defy convention and comfort and demand that readers summon the courage to explore. At the same time, literary words are not ordinary words, and the series implicitly raises the question of how literature can be delineated and delimited. While *Mingling Voices* welcomes original work—poems, short stories, and, on occasion, novels—written in English, it also acknowledges the craft of translators, who build bridges across the borders of language. Similarly, the series is interested in cultural crossings, whether through immigration or travel or through the interweaving of literary traditions themselves.

Series Titles

Poems for a Small Park
E.D. Blodgett

Dreamwork
Jonathan Locke Hart

Windfall Apples: Tanka and Kyoka
Richard Stevenson

Zeus and the Giant Iced Tea
Leopold McGinnis

Praha
E.D. Blodgett

The Metabolism of Desire:
The Poetry of Guido Cavalcanti
Translated by David R. Slavitt

kiyâm
Naomi McIlwraith

Sefer
Ewa Lipska, translated by Barbara Bogoczek and Tony Howard

Spark of Light: Short Stories by Women Writers of Odisha
Edited by Valerie Henitiuk and Supriya Kar

Kaj Smo, Ko Smo /
What We Are When We Are
Cvetka Lipuš, Translation by Tom Priestly

From Turtle Island to Gaza
David Groulx

from
TURTLE *to*
ISLAND GAZA

David Groulx

AU PRESS

© 2019 David Groulx

Published by AU Press, Athabasca University

1200, 10011 – 109 Street, Edmonton, AB T5J 3S8

ISBN 978-1-77199-261-9 (pbk)   ISBN 978-1-77199-262-6 (pdf)
ISBN 978-1-77199-263-3 (epub)   doi:10.15215/aupress/9781771992619.01

Some of this work has appeared in *Grey Borders* and *Rabbit: A Journal for Nonfiction Poetry*.

Cover design by Natalie Olsen, kisscutdesign.com
Interior design by Sergiy Kozakov
Printed and bound in Canada

Library and Archives Canada Cataloguing in Publication

Groulx, David, 1969–, author.
    From Turtle Island to Gaza / David Groulx.
(Mingling voices)
Poems.
Issued in print and electronic formats.

Canadiana (print) 20190064765 | Canadiana (ebook) 20190064781
LCC PS8563.R76 F76 2019   DDC C811/.54—dc23

We acknowledge the financial support of the Government of Canada through the Canada Book Fund (CBF) for our publishing activities and the assistance provided by the Government of Alberta through the Alberta Media Fund.

Canadä
Alberta
Government

Preface

I began writing *From Turtle Island to Gaza* in 2016, but the idea came to me several years earlier at a poetry reading in Toronto's Harbourfront, where I was reading from *A Difficult Beauty*. In the poem "Widening the Highway on the Rez" are the lines, "now this land becomes our Palestine / broken off from torso and limb / this long execution." After the reading, an older Palestinian man joined me for a smoke outside, and he told me how much he loved these lines. We spoke very little, as we both knew we shared that long execution—that distance, religion, education could not break what we shared. Colonialism is a shared experience. I've always known that, and I've always known that the Indigenous peoples here on Turtle Island were not the first or the only peoples to endure this long execution. I wanted to make what we have experienced here available to the world, believing that sharing stories is a power more powerful than bombs, bullets, or religion.

Some of the pieces address Palestinian poets—Mourid Barghouti, Mahmoud Darwish, Suheir Hammad, Rashid Hussein, Salma Jayyusi, Samih al-Qasim, Anton Shammas, Fadwa Tuqan, and Ibrahim Tuqan—I list their names here so you may hear them too.

In these poems I hope we find that we, colonized peoples, are not alone.

My
wing high
breaking distance
my voice
the sorrow
on the land
of a people.
A blood mercy.

Beneath the snow
I sing a new note
taste a winter
coming
on my Circean tongue
Red River
wheels
escape.
I rekindle.

The days of October
my wings will lyric
and sway
for six days
I am crossing
a green line

I am wearing
a blue line
across the desert sky
I braid the light
across the desert earth

My loom
has become
black dust.
My wreaths
become
blood.

I know not
to cry
while the rockets
bluster
and the snow
gruff and deep.
This fine white garment
clothes the earth.

We are like the
wholeness of the sun
the light sinks
into the
earth.
Ritual
Remains.

We are the road
allowance nation
it is our Ghazze
here we live
our songs
live.

Sing now
to what is broken
lift your kisses
bring mercy
and raise us
from our
slumber.

The spring is always
clouded
with snow
ah, the dust
of an angry
bolt
faithful
to bring
weeping.

Sing me Fanon
Sing me inferno
Your
oscine shiver
over the catatonic
sleep of
Île-à-la-Crosse
and the Cedars
of Lebanon

Fly over the
broken peace
wave your bloody
wings
call the seditious
the intifada
serve our portion
of Azrael's sickle.

The monster's skin
a pall of shit
Its bloating corpse
choking on
Apician graces

I was Majdal
now I am Ashkelon
the ground
cursed by God
is settled
becomes unsettled.

The earth becomes twisted
beneath the wheel
the wheel
scars
the earth.
What was
Red River
crumbles
beneath.

The snow has fallen
and fallen
over Mount Tabor
over *Ansar* thee
now we are off the land
and held in acres of misery

Winter crumbles
with what's left
grinds into the earth
A new corpse of spring.

This place was called
'Ayn Hawd
now it is Ein Hod
the settlers
live there now
painting pictures
writing stories
our lives are
silent.

Who will carry on the war?
that we made
that we live
Who will carry on the war?
when we go
into the bowels of our
enemy.
Who will finish
the slaughter?

Dance with me once more
show me where the worm
the vulture
and the maggot
feast
Scatter my flowers
that were gathered
by this wretched beast
Milkweed grows over
my garden earth and butterflies
pass into the earth.

I've been invited
to leave my country
as you have yours
Shammas
perhaps we could
leave
together
We sacred kings

Find a new country
to bury our dead
leave the land
of your pilgrimage
I leave the land
to the white settlers

Where should we go?
You and I
Where can we go?
We, Refuge
refuge *refuse*
from the occupied

We become aliens
strangers
outsiders
foreigners
unknown
in our own land
other

Samih
this soil is sacred
like water
My land is holy
too
and
from it
I cannot be severed

It is Canada day here
Samih
everyone is happy
because it's a holiday
I do not know
what to feel

The land becomes pale
and the birds
do not recognize
it
the birds
sing
the land is
silent
barren
with no reply

Rashid
there is a Settler's daughter
in a headdress
a star of David
in her mouth
her hands wrapped
in barbed wire

Dear Mahmoud
Here I am
without our lives
we live in prisons
of poverty
behind walls of despair
but fortunately Mahmoud
we do not live long.

All I can do
when I see a policeman
is growl
under my breath
this is all
I can do

When we speak of freedom
we must also speak of our freedom
to be kind
to be just
and to be in love
when we speak of freedom
this is what we
must speak of

The Lakota call
white people Wasi'chu
meaning *steals the fat*.
The Anishinaabeg call
white people Zhaaganaash
meaning *fell from the sky*.
White people call us Indians
because they think
they are in India.

The language I speak
are the walls of my prison
the language I speak are
the bars of my prison
The words I speak
are a history of the
death of language.

If we know our oppressor
lives in prisons of anger
How can the settler
be our master?

Israel has built a wall around itself
a narrow prison.
Past the wall
the earth swallows
lentils
and boiled eggs

Mahmoud
Men will use anything to take our land
Guns, bombs, swords.
The word of God, but mostly
the twisted word
of God.

The earth has been untied from me
untied from my barbarian heart
untied from my black ash hair.
My bone has become untied from my skin.
My mouth untied from my tongue.
Now only the earth grows in my ear.

Today Mahmoud
I worked all day in the freezing rain
shoveling snow
from foundations.
The day was cold,
but I can think of
others
that made me old.

The history books say
you left Al-Tira
willingly.
Mortars and machine guns
can do this.
A bullet has a way of
convincing like no other.
We know my friend
that bullets and bombs
cannot kill
the dirt that runs
through our veins.

I live under this iron
where there are two goats
one is black, one is white
One is given to the lord
The other to the valley
I follow the one
that is lost

We are stuck in the throat
of a settler.
Like a chicken bone from a
hen whose throat has been slit
and yet bleeds in the barnyard.

A Windigo is not a djinn
My dear friend
A Windigo was once a man
with an unquenchable appetite.
That he craved the flesh of Indians.
but you and I know
it is our land.

Is suicide as common there as it is
here? Mahmoud.
I knew a young Indian boy once,
he found his oldest sister
hanging in his closet
dead.
After her funeral
his younger sister hung herself also.
The boy doused himself in gasoline
and lit himself on fire
and the ice was thin enough he fell through
No the young boy was not a phoenix.
He did not rise up out of the ashes.
Those are only stories.
This one I could touch.
He was only a young Native boy.
I cry Mahmoud, when I remember
it.

Is suicide as normal there
as it is here, Mahmoud?

I am closer to Rome
than you are
I see its flickering lights at night
I hear the fighter jets ringing toward you
see the tanks rolling toward you
the warships lifting anchor
do not go to Damascus
do not go to Beirut
do not go to God
it is not safe there.
You are closer to Rome
than I am

The siege came to us
and forced us off the land.
The siege then taught us English
and left us speechless.
The siege showed us its riches
and left us in poverty.
The siege dragged us to its school
and left us wretched.
The siege taught us its work
and left us unemployed.
The siege taught us its war
and left us murdered.
Buried us in heaps
and forgets
about us.

The missing are prisoners of our
memory.
Our leaders bray like donkeys
to the settler.
I write poems no one reads,
and the settler feeds them more carrots.

That woman of Rome
We carry her on our shoulders, you
and I.
It is our business, our
bread and butter.
Her wounded border, where
daylight escapes and night time
enters, our bellies
drag us along.

This soil
in my palms
was the place of God
howling
to the four directions

This soil
is his flesh
He cannot abandon it.

*And Samson said, "Let me die with the
    Philistines."* Judges 16:30 (KJV)
Call out to God
That I may leave
my thunder and lightning on this earth
peace be upon him.
That I may
lay the broken jawbone
and broken pillars
here in the grace
of Canaan.

Mourid you said it was fine to die on a
clean white pillow
You said it was fine to die of old age
is this what I am afraid of ?
I dream I am drowning in the rivers of the
    country
That someone is holding me there
Here is a clean white pillow
beneath the currents

Hold me Fadwa
because we know
memory knows no compromise
The blood does not negotiate
The songs of our ancestors will not make us
or our oppressor comfortable

Salma
If Palestine was the size of Canada
they would have put you on reservations far
    off in the bush
away
so they didn't have to look at you
didn't have to see any of your number
didn't have to see the suicide of your children
After all they are only brown
after all
Let you die there dirt poor
without any clean water to drink or bathe in
    and then say don't look at those
dirty Palestinians
They are poor and dirty
in the land god gave to us
and the land god gave to you
they say god gave to them
as if god is only books and bullets

Our lives are unpalatable to them
and then they claim they had nothing to do
    with it
It was God
Suheir
It was always God

Name your oppressors Ibrahim
create a space with your words and whisper it
    to me
and we can share it and
in this space
together create hope.
The sound of the name
creates hope.
Hope that begins
breaking at the first word
like dawn.